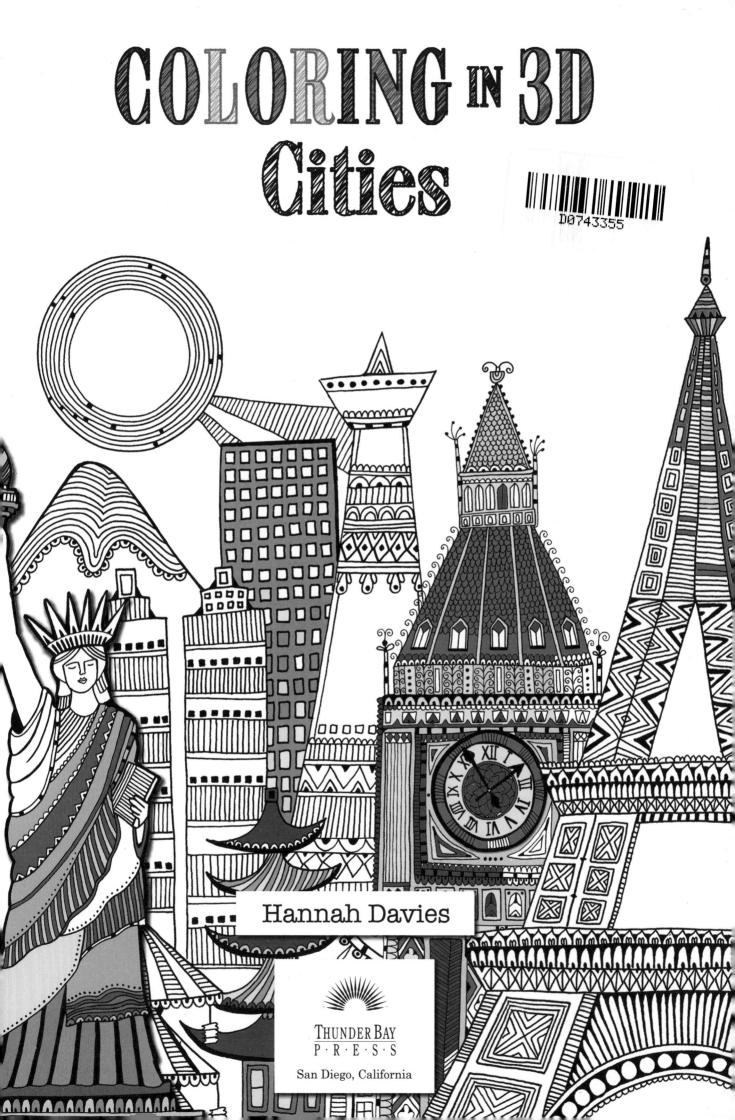

COLORING IN 3D
Cities

Hannah Davies

THUNDER BAY
P·R·E·S·S

San Diego, California

Thunder Bay Press
An imprint of Printers Row Publishing Group
10350 Barnes Canyon Road, Suite 100
San Diego, CA 92121
www.thunderbaybooks.com

This book was conceived, designed, and produced by
Quintet Publishing Limited
114–116 Western Road
Hove, East Sussex
BN3 1DD
United Kingdom

QTT.3DCI4

Thunder Bay Team:
Publisher: Peter Norton
Publishing Team: Lori Asbury, Ana Parker, Laura Vignale
Editorial Team: JoAnn Padgett, Melinda Allman, Traci Douglas

Quintet Publishing Team:
Project Editors: Alice Sambrook, Leah Feltham
Designers: Gareth Butterworth, Paula Lewis, Ian Miller
Illustrator: Hannah Davies
Art Director: Michael Charles
Publisher: Mark Searle

ISBN: 978-1-62686-669-0

Printed and bound in China by RR Donnelley

20 19 18 17 16   1 2 3 4 5

The glasses included with this book are intended only for viewing ChromaDepth® 3D images. Not for extended wear, performing physical activity, driving, or operating machinery. Do not look into the sun with glasses. Manufactured by American Paper Optics, LLC, Bartlett, Tennessee, USA.

This book belongs to

....

CONTENTS

Introduction 5

How to color in 3D 6

Toronto, CN Tower 8

Havana, Cuba 10

Montreal, Biosphère 12

New York, Statue of Liberty 13

Seattle...14

New York, Central Park 16

Lima..18

Las Vegas 20

New Orleans, Saint Louis Cathedral ...21

San Francisco 22

Jodhpur, India 24

Savannah, Georgia 26

Rio de Janeiro, Christ the Redeemer ...28

Los Angeles..30

London, Big Ben..31

Edinburgh, Scotland, Edinburgh International Conference Centre...........32

London, the Shard....................................34

Paris, Arc de Triomphe 35

Dublin..36

Paris, Eiffel Tower 38

Rome, St. Peter's Basilica 39

Seville...40

Barcelona, Sagrada Familia 42

Yangon, Myanmar 44

Berlin, Television Tower 46

Madrid, The ABC Museum 47

Chiang Mai, Thailand...............................48

Amsterdam 50

Samarkand, Uzbekistan 52

Istanbul 54

Mumbai...56

Giza...58

Budapest, Parliament Building 60

Kyoto..62

Stockholm...64

Krakow...65

Moscow, The Kremlin 66

Cape Town..68

Shanghai, The Oriental Pearl Tower 70

Hong Kong 72

Siem Reap, Cambodia, The Angkor Temples 74

Tokyo, Mount Fuji 76

Sydney, Opera House...............................78

Auckland, Sky Tower.................................80

INTRODUCTION

I grew up beside the sea in south Wales. It's a beautiful part of the world with areas of outstanding natural beauty. Spending all these years here has made me the person I am today: creative, colorful, and absolutely obsessed with drawing.

The beaches are untouched, and there are miles of landscape to explore. I walk these beaches twice a day with my Old English Sheepdog, Charlie, and see so many changes in water patterns, waves, tides, sunsets, and sunrises, and also spectacular full moons. The inspirational happenings in nature encourage me to draw day and night, and I can't imagine a day without doodling. If ever you need artistic incentive, I would advise getting outside and absorbing the world around you.

I am fascinated with microscopic patterns and detail, and love creating endless layers and textures, which you will see reflected in the pages of this book. It is a collection of reconceived iconic landmarks, urban metropolises, and sprawling cityscapes from my imagination! Hopefully, these drawings will inspire you to create designs of your own.

You can then use your 3D glasses to see the patterns and scenes pop off the page as you color them in. I would suggest applying vibrant watercolor pencils to get the best effect, but felt-tip pens are fine too. I hope that this book gives you as much enjoyment experimenting as I have had creating it. Happy coloring in 3D!

If you love this book, why not try out the others in the series, *Coloring in 3D Flowers* and *Coloring in 3D Animals?*

H Davies

HOW TO COLOR IN 3D

Included in this book, you will find a pair of ChromaDepth® 3D glasses that use the latest in stereoscopic technology to create an amazing illusion of depth in hand-drawn images.

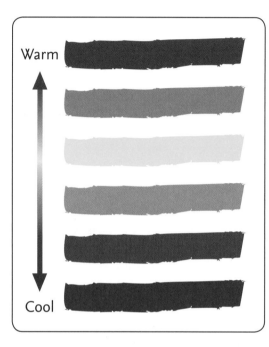

- Use cool colors for parts that you want to banish to the background. Use warm colors for parts of a drawing that you want to come forward and appear as if they are floating up off the page.

- Follow the color chart at the left if you need a quick reminder of what cool and warm colors are.

- Whether you pick out small details and bring these to the foreground or choose to feature larger areas does not matter. It's all about experimenting to see what looks groovy.

- Get inspired and create your own illustrations.

Note
We recommend that you use bright watercolor pencils or felt-tip pens to achieve the best possible effect.

Tips

Tint

Bold, bright colors appear the most 3D. The lighter the colors, the more they will lie toward the middle of the spectrum and will neither jump forward nor move back much at all. However, you can use lighter tints effectively alongside bold colors to add texture to dark backgrounds.

Depth perception and shading

It is possible to enhance the 3D effect created by the glasses by using standard artistic techniques. Use shading to emphasize roundness and shadows to exaggerate overlapping objects. Create a sense of depth through the use of bright colors on foreground objects.

Use of black

Black tends to complement cool and warm colors alike. 3D images would not appear so without the use of black outlines; without them, the colors inhabit an undefined area. Black outlines provide edges for your mind to locate in space, enlarging the apparent depth. Use thicker black outlines for the areas you want to really pop.

Use of white

Whereas black is happy to sit at the front or back of a 3D image, white will always appear in the middleground. This can be useful to provide a central horizon for the warm and cool colors to stand on either side of. Be careful when touching warm colors to the white border though; it may drag them back from the foreground.

15

23

33

38

41

46

69